Beginning Fiddle Duets

for two violas

Book One

written and arranged by Myanna Harvey

CHP304

©2016 by C. Harvey Publications All Rights Reserved.

www.charveypublications.com - print books
www.Learnstrings.com - PDF downloadable books
www.harveystringarrangements.com - chamber music

Beginning Fiddle Duets for Two Violas

Written and arranged by Myanna Harvey

Table of Contents

Title	Page
1. Cripple Creek	2
2. Bingo	4
3. Drill Ye Tarriers	5
4. Old Joe Clark	6
5. Erie Canal	8
6. Arkansas Traveler	10
7. I Ride an Old Paint	11
8. Battle Cry of Freedom	12
9. Goober Peas	14
10. Aiken Drum	16
11. Sailor's Jig	18
12. The Muffin Man	20
13. Oh Susannah	22
14. Yankee Doodle	24
15. The Horse and the Flea	26
16. Piper's Jig	28
17. Camptown Races	30
18. Kentucky Lullaby	32

©2016 by C. Harvey Publications All Rights Reserved.

Beginning Fiddle Duets for Two Violas

Cripple Creek

Trad., arr. Myanna Harvey

©2016 C. Harvey Publications All Rights Reserved.

Beginning Fiddle Duets for Two Violas

Bingo

Trad., arr. Myanna Harvey

©2016 C. Harvey Publications All Rights Reserved.

Drill Ye Tarriers

Trad., arr. Myanna Harvey

©2016 C. Harvey Publications All Rights Reserved.

Old Joe Clark

Trad., arr. Myanna Harvey

©2016 C. Harvey Publications All Rights Reserved.

Erie Canal

Trad., arr. Myanna Harvey

©2016 C. Harvey Publications All Rights Reserved.

Beginning Fiddle Duets for Two Violas

©2016 C. Harvey Publications All Rights Reserved.

Arkansas Traveler

Trad., arr. Myanna Harvey

©2016 C. Harvey Publications All Rights Reserved.

I Ride an Old Paint

Trad., arr. Myanna Harvey

©2016 C. Harvey Publications All Rights Reserved.

Battle Cry of Freedom

Trad., arr. Myanna Harvey

©2016 C. Harvey Publications All Rights Reserved.

Beginning Fiddle Duets for Two Violas

©2016 C. Harvey Publications All Rights Reserved.

Goober Peas

Trad., arr. Myanna Harvey

Beginning Fiddle Duets for Two Violas

Aiken Drum

Trad., arr. Myanna Harvey

©2016 C. Harvey Publications All Rights Reserved.

Beginning Fiddle Duets for Two Violas

Sailor's Jig

Myanna Harvey

©2016 C. Harvey Publications All Rights Reserved.

Beginning Fiddle Duets for Two Violas

The Muffin Man

Trad., arr. Myanna Harvey

©2016 C. Harvey Publications All Rights Reserved.

Beginning Fiddle Duets for Two Violas

Oh Susannah

Foster, arr. Myanna Harvey

©2016 C. Harvey Publications All Rights Reserved.

Beginning Fiddle Duets for Two Violas

Yankee Doodle

Trad., arr. Myanna Harvey

©2016 C. Harvey Publications All Rights Reserved.

Beginning Fiddle Duets for Two Violas

The Horse and the Flea

Trad., arr. Myanna Harvey

©2016 C. Harvey Publications All Rights Reserved.

Beginning Fiddle Duets for Two Violas

Piper's Jig

Myanna Harvey

Beginning Fiddle Duets for Two Violas

29

Camptown Races

Foster., arr. Myanna Harvey

Beginning Fiddle Duets for Two Violas

Kentucky Lullaby

Trad., arr. Myanna Harvey

©2016 C. Harvey Publications All Rights Reserved.

Beginning Fiddle Duets for Two Violas

available from **www.charveypublications.com**: CHP268

Flying Fiddle Duets for Two Violas, Book One

John Ryan's Polka

Trad., arr. Myanna Harvey

©2015 C. Harvey Publications. All Rights Reserved.

www.ingramcontent.com/pod-product-compliance
Lightning Source LLC
Chambersburg PA
CBHW051427070526
44584CB00023B/3617